THE TRUST

# TRUST

# ADMINISTRATION

## *in*

# CALIFORNIA

BRENDA GEIGER, J.D.

GEIGER LAW OFFICE, P.C.

www.geigerlawoffice.com

1917 Palomar Oaks Way, Suite 160
Carlsbad, CA 92008
**(760) 448-2220**

16A Journey, Suite. 200
Aliso Viejo, CA 92656
**(949) 769-2440**

Printed in the United States of America.

ISBN:  978-1-63385-304-1   [paperback]
ISBN:  978-1-63385-305-8   [hardback]


*Designed and published by*

Word Association Publishers
205 Fifth Avenue
Tarentum, Pennsylvania 15084

www.wordassociation.com
1.800.827.7903

# CONTENTS

# CHAPTER ONE

# Introduction
# to Trust Administration
# in California

WHEN A LOVED ONE DIES and they have a trust, the process of trust administration will need to be undertaken. Many lawyers make trust administration appear simple at the time their client signs the trust document without fully explaining what will need to happen after their death. This is dangerous because often the client never discusses trust administration with their Successor Trustee. The person or people that will serve as Trustee need to understand what should happen at the time of death of the person creating the trust.

Over the years, it has been our experience that sometimes clients have unrealistic expectations about how their trust will work when a death occurs. The most common misconceptions are that everything will happen "automatically" and that the assistance of an attorney and CPA is not necessary to administer the trust.

There are administrative duties and expenses involved in trust administration that families and Trustees need to understand. One of the most frequent misunderstandings happens when there is a joint trust between a husband and a wife and the trust provisions call for the trust to be split at the time the first spouse dies (often between a Survivor's Trust and a Bypass Trust or QTIP Trust). The most common reasons for having these types of trusts are for estate tax savings for larger estates, asset protection for the surviving spouse, and divorce-remarriage protection for the first to die's half of the estate. It is key to remember that by having a trust, the individual or couple that set up the trust will avoid probate (provided the trust was properly funded) and there could be estate tax or capital gains tax savings as a byproduct of the estate plan.

The language in a joint marital trust can be quite confusing to read and interpret. Make sure you consult a qualified Estate Attorney who can help you understand your legal obligations in administering the trust.

If there is a call for a division of the trust or allocation into sub-trusts for beneficiaries, typically, the first thing that happens is an "administrative" trust with its own tax identification number that needs to be set up. This is for accounting purposes. The trust usually allows for the payment the funeral expenses, taxes, outstanding bills, and last illness expenses of the deceased Grantor. Other administrative expenses like, attorney fees and CPA fees are also commonly covered expenses in the trust. The successor Trustee will usually set up a new bank account in the name of the "administrative" trust to track all expenses using a new tax identification number obtained from the IRS. The chapters that follow are designed to help you understand the big picture of a trust administration and provide you with some practical tips to help you avoid being sued by a beneficiary and keep you out of hot water with the IRS and California Franchise Tax Board.

# CHAPTER TWO

# Checklist
## for What to Do After the Death of a Loved One

## IMMEDIATELY:

❏ Inform family and friends. Ask other family members for help planning funeral or celebration of life services.

❏ Contact funeral home, cemetery, crematorium or whomever is taking the body according to the deceased's wishes (if any).

❏ If the deceased's wishes are unknown, decide on disposition of remains and purchase an urn or casket as necessary.

❏ If the deceased was religiously affiliated, contact their parish, congregation, mosque or synagogue.

❏ Arrange for funeral or celebration of life services:

❏ (A) Be sure to check the deceased's Estate Plan binder for any specific memorial instructions, paid burial plots or prepaid funeral plans.

❏ (B) Order flowers.

❏ (C) Inform friends and family of the date and time of the funeral or celebration of life services.

❏ (D) Create a picture board or video stream of the deceased to display at the funeral home, church and/or celebration of life service site.

❏ (E) Design memorial cards to be distributed at any services being held.

❏ (F) If applicable, choose music, songs or hymns where the services are being held.

❏ (G) Choose pallbearer's or other family or friends who will be helping assist in any church, funeral home or celebration of life services.

❏ (H) Create obituary and send to local newspaper, funeral home and/or wherever else you'd like to see the obituary posted. Include the deceased's name, age, city of residence, date of death, birthplace and year of birth, who they are survived by, and a brief summary of who they were (for example, explain their life's work, priorities, life philosophy, etc.). Also, include any details of the funeral service or celebration of life service, if any. Note: funeral homes are often willing to help you create this if you ask.

❏ (I) When appropriate, post on social media about the death, but do not do so until all immediate family members have been notified.

❏ (J) Notify any employers or business partners of the deceased's death.

## THE NEXT 1-2 WEEKS:

❏ Notify Social Security of the death to stop any social security payments. Most funeral homes do this as a courtesy so it is smart to inquire. If social security deposits a direct payment to the deceased's checking account after they died or sends them a check, you will need to return that check or direct deposit to the Social Security Administration. Social Security Administration: 1-800-772-1213. Note: once Social Security is aware of the death, they will usually automatically reverse a direct deposit for any payments that were made to the decedent's bank account after death.

❏ If you are the Trustee and/or Executor of the deceased's estate, contact the post office to change the deceased's mailing address to your address so that you get all of the deceased's mail moving forward.

❏ Contact an experienced Estate Attorney to administer the trust and/or to open up a Probate Court case to settle the estate. Make an appointment with them before moving any assets around. There are many rules and deadlines in a trust administration or Probate case. **Seek counsel early to ensure all rules and deadlines are met and to protect yourself as Trustee or Executor from lawsuits or IRS claims.**

❏ Notify the deceased's financial advisor and CPA, if known. Advise them of the death and connect them with the Estate Attorney.

❏ Collect all of the estate planning documents and asset information of the deceased and send them to the Estate Attorney for review before your scheduled meeting.

# ASSET INFORMATION TO COLLECT AND SEND TO THE ESTATE ATTORNEY:

❏ (A) Collect any information on life insurance benefits of any kind.

❏ (B) Obtain IRA, 401(k), 403B, and any other retirement account beneficiary designation forms and/or copies of most recent account statements.

❏ (C) Obtain copies of any real estate property deeds (the attorney can usually obtain them if you cannot locate them).

❏ (D) Obtain copies of the most recent bank statements for all bank accounts.

❏ (E) Obtain copies of pink slips to any vehicles owned by the deceased.

❏ (F) Obtain copies of the most recent account statements for any non-retirement brokerage accounts.

❏ (G) Obtain copies of any corporate, LLC or partnership interest records for business interests held by the deceased.

❑ (H) Obtain copies of any other investment information such as deeds of trust, notes or other loans owed to the deceased (if any).

❑ (I) Create a list of all <u>known</u> creditors and liabilities of the deceased.

❑ (J) Obtain the last 2 years tax returns, if available, and name of the deceased's CPA, if known.

❑ Order 5 to 10 Certified Death Certificates — the funeral home can typically help you with this.

❑ Contact the DMV to cancel the driver's license of the deceased (bring the death certificate to the DMV with you).

❑ Monitor the deceased's credit report for any suspicious activity after death (there are identity thieves that can reek havoc on a deceased's person's credit report). See www.myfico.com.

## NEXT 2-4 WEEKS:

❑ If the deceased had a safety deposit box, go to the bank to access the box if you are a signor on the box and you have a key to inventory the contents of the box. <u>Report inventory to attorney</u>. If you do not have access to the box, the attorney may need to petition the court to allow you to have access.

❏ Apply for Social Security Survivor benefits, if applicable. Most of the time this is applicable if you are the surviving spouse.

❏ Collect any Veteran's Administration benefits (if applicable). You will need military honorable discharge paperwork of the deceased. Contact online at www.va.gov or call 1-800-827-1000.

❏ Continue paying all recurring bills related to the deceased, keep receipts and track if you are paying out of pocket so that you can be reimbursed from the deceased's estate. To the extent possible, pay all bills and expenses from the deceased's trust bank account(s).

❏ Check for any upcoming travel plans of the deceased and cancel or transfer all flights or car reservations.

❏ Organize bills, payments, statements and financial information in a tabbed binder for organized access. Place all new statements under the appropriate tab as they are received.

❏ Obtain date-of-death values on all accounts and properties for basis adjustment.

❏ If there are survivors of the deceased, ensure continuing coverage for health care, disability, long-term care, auto insurance, homeowners' insurance, and umbrella insurance, or life insurance (if applicable). Cancel any coverage that is no longer necessary.

❏ If the deceased was a renter, inform the landlord of the death and work towards moving all personal belongings out of the property and into a secure storage facility.

❏ If need be, hold an estate sale and/or donate items that family does not need or want. But be sure to check the Will or Trust for direction on distribution of personal property. It is best to ask your Estate Attorney for guidance here. For a referral to a professional to help hold the estate sale, call our main office at (760) 448-2220.

❏ Write thank you notes to anyone who has helped or donated time, flowers or other gifts to the family.

❏ Cancel any credit cards or recurring subscriptions in the name of the deceased.

❏ Continue working with the Estate Attorney on the settlement process including the retitling of any vehicles, real estate, bank or investment accounts and any other accounts to the name of the new Trustee.

❏ Work with the Estate Attorney and financial advisor concerning all rollovers of IRAs and/or other retirement accounts or pensions. There are deadlines for these types of transactions to ensure stretch-out for non-spouse beneficiaries and to withdraw the deceased's annual required minimum distribution (in some cases).

❏ Discuss with the Estate Attorney the IRS guidelines for filing an estate tax return (whether needed or not) as well as the final tax return for the deceased and any required 1041 trust tax returns. Coordinate with CPA.

## IN THE MONTHS THAT FOLLOW:

❏ Decide what to do with the deceased's social media content, if any. Think Facebook, LinkedIn, Instagram, Google, Twitter, to name a few. Cancel online banking, PayPal, etc. where accounts and logins are known.

❏ If the deceased owned a business, work on succession and continuity plans, selling the business, or closing the company. Work with the Estate Attorney to this end.

❏ Create or update your own estate planning documents. This is important so that you remain in control of your medical treatment and finances through your selected agents should you ever be unable to act for yourself. This will also ensure less arguments and guilt among your loved ones because they won't have to make difficult decisions without knowing what you wanted and who you wanted to take care of it.

❏ Annually review, and if necessary, update your trust beneficiaries, Trustees and agents on your other estate planning documents.

If you are the Trustee or Executor of a loved one's estate and you need assistance in settling the estate, call, text or email our office at (760) 448-2220 (lisa@geigerlawoffice.com) to discuss how we may be able to assist you and protect you from any liability claims in the process of settling the estate.

Our intake team is here to assist you in your time of need.

# CHAPTER THREE

# Your Responsibilities as Trustee

THERE ARE MANY THINGS that can happen in a trust administration and many duties that the Trustee could be responsible for.

## SOME OF THESE THINGS COULD INCLUDE:

1. Notifying trust beneficiaries and heirs at law of the death of the trust Grantor (this involves a legal notice in California);

2. Obtaining IRS Tax ID Number(s) for the trust and/or sub-trusts;

3. Filing a final income tax return for the decedent;

4. Filing a death tax return;

5. Filing a trust income tax return annually for as long as the trust is held open;

6. Publishing a legal notice with the Court and in a local newspaper regarding the death of the Grantor of the trust;

7. Marshalling all of the assets together and protecting the trust assets;

8. Depositing the decedent's original Will with the Court;
9. Opening a bank account for the trust;
10. Transferring title of the deceased assets to the name of the Trustee for management during administration;
11. Paying financial and last illness expenses of the decedent;
12. Collecting life insurance policy proceeds;
13. Determining if a formal Probate or other legal action needs to be taken for any assets not titled in the name of the trust;
14. Notifying all banks and financial institutions of the death and that you are the nominated Successor Trustee;
15. Notifying the Veteran's Administration (if applicable) and Department of Health Services of the death;
16. Determining beneficiary status of all the decedent's retirement accounts and life insurance. For most 401Ks and IRAs, a stretch out is available for a non-spousal beneficiary if the proper steps are taken within the prescribed time period (note that this can be a huge tax advantage);
17. Obtaining date-of-death valuations on all assets and property of the decedent including real estate and business interests;
18. Determining if an estate tax is due on the decedent's Estate;
19. Paying off all of the debts of the Grantor from the assets of the trust;

20. Paying ongoing expenses of trust administration such as legal and CPA expenses, taxes, etc.;

21. Liquidating assets when necessary to pay off the debts of the Grantor (but with tax and legal advice first);

22. Investing assets of the trust in a safe and prudent manner during trust administration;

23. Determining if a Parent/Child Exclusion from real estate tax reassessment should be filed with the County Recorder's Office;

24. Distributing the trust assets to the beneficiaries or to trusts set up for the benefit of the beneficiaries after all of the above has been completed.

Note that the above list is NOT an exhaustive list. There are often additional considerations and tasks in an estate that need to be legally analyzed and dealt with. The above examples are simply a list of some of the common items a Trustee might be called to do.

Also, it is important to note that each trust is unique and the situation, beneficiaries and assets of the Grantor of that trust are unique. So some things that may not occur in one trust administration may need to occur in another. Therefore, it is important to hire an experienced Estate Attorney in your administration of the trust. This can also help shield you from an IRS attack or expensive and stressful lawsuit from a beneficiary.

# CHAPTER FOUR

# Do's & Don'ts
# in Trust Administration

THE FOLLOWING IS A LIST of do's and don'ts to pay particular attention to before you get started with any trust administration.

## DO'S

1.  Do take your role as Trustee seriously.
2.  Do seek the guidance and advice of a qualified Estate Attorney, accountant and financial advisor.
3.  Do get and stay organized with all the paperwork and financial record keeping involved in settling an estate.
4.  Do run all trust transactions through a bank or brokerage account that is titled in the name of the trust.
5.  Do maintain paper records of all financial and legal records related to the trust.
6.  Do document all meetings and phone calls with your Estate Attorney, CPA, financial advisor and with the beneficiaries.
7.  Do maintain confidentiality regarding trust matters but make sure to inform the trust beneficiaries from

time to time about the status of the settlement of the trust estate. You do want to be responsive to their questions and requests in order to lower any risk of future lawsuits against you as the Trustee.

8.   Do remember that it is always better to act slowly and cautiously instead of quickly and/or aggressively and with sound legal and tax advice.

## DON'TS

1.   Don't ignore the IRS. There are filing deadlines for the decedent as well as the trust. Most of the time these deadlines coincide with the general April 15th tax filing deadline for income tax returns. However, if a 706 death tax return is required or recommended, that deadline is nine months after the date of death of the decedent.

2.   Don't immediately start cashing out assets, selling properties or reinvesting assets. There could be serious tax consequences that are presently unknown to you. Consult with an experienced Estate Attorney and a CPA before taking action.

3.   Don't attempt to interpret legal language. When it comes to the law, it is a language in and of itself. What a passage in a trust or will means legally may be far different than your interpretation of it. Consult an experienced Estate Attorney to help with interpreting the trust.

4.   Don't cash out the IRA, 401K or other qualified retirement accounts. If you do, you will blow any oppor-

tunity for tax deferral and stretch out of the account. Discuss this with an experienced Estate Attorney and CPA before taking any action.

5. Don't commingle Trust funds with your own or use any Trust Assets for your own personal purposes or expenses. You have a fiduciary duty as Trustee to the trust beneficiaries.

6. Don't make loans to anyone from Trust funds without first consulting an attorney.

7. Don't represent yourself if a beneficiary becomes represented by an attorney. Seek legal counsel immediately if this occurs.

8. Don't forget to check to see when the local real estate tax deadlines are when the trust owns real property (normally they are December 10th and April 10th).

9. Don't act alone if there is another Trustee listed as a Co-Trustee with you.

10. Don't ignore correspondence from the beneficiaries or their legal counsel, the IRS or Franchise Tax Board, attorneys or CPAs.

# CHAPTER FIVE

# *Estate Taxes*

EFFECTIVE AS OF JANUARY 1, 2018, the Tax Cuts and Jobs Act of 2017 changed the Federal Estate Tax exemption rate. In 2019, that exemption increased to $11,400,000 per person and is indexed for inflation each year. This number represents the unified credit amount that each U.S. Citizen can gift during their lifetime, transfer at death or apply to generation-skipping transfers (transfers to someone more than one generation removed). All three are under one unified combined credit.

For example, if Tom gave his child $2MM during his lifetime, his credit would be reduced by $2MM to $9,400,000 if he died in 2019 for death-time and/or generation-skipping transfers. Estate, Gift and Generation-Skipping Transfer Taxes under the current law are unified (made the same). This means that the estate and gift taxes create a single graduated exemption rate schedule for both estate and gift taxes.

The single lifetime exemption can be used for lifetime gifts, death-time bequests and generation-skipping transfers. The top estate and gift tax rates are 40% for transfers of assets beyond the $11,400,000 exemption (2019). What this means is that starting in 2019, each U.S. citizen may transfer up to $11,400,000 throughout his or her lifetime or at death (or some combination thereof) and not be subject to estate or gift taxes.

The exemption that applies to a decedent is the exemption that is in effect in the year he or she dies. A married couple with community property assets may transfer up to $22,800,000 (2019) since each spouse has their own exemption. Special rules apply for estates involving non-US citizen spouses, so consultation with an experienced estate planning attorney is strongly recommended.

It is also important to note that the estate tax provisions of the Tax Cuts and Jobs Act of 2017 are set to sunset (expire) at the end of 2025. This means that absent of further legislation, on January 1, 2026 the estate tax exemption will fall back to the Pre-Jobs Act exemption amount of $5,000,000 per person (indexed annually for inflation).

Two final notes. First, California does not have an estate tax. Second, upon the death of one spouse, if there are no marital trusts set up in the joint revocable trust to allocate the deceased spouse's estate tax exemption to, it may be advisable to file a 706 death tax return. This is important to preserve the "portability" of the deceased spouse's exemption. The deadline to file a 706 death tax return is within nine months from the date of death of the decedent. Whether or not a death tax return should be filed is a detailed discussion that should happen with an experienced Estate Attorney and should occur well in advance of the deadline.

# CHAPTER SIX

# *The Fiduciary Duties of the Trustee*

TRUSTEES OWE A GREAT RESPONSIBILITY not only to the person who created the trust, but also to the beneficiaries of the trust. In the legal context, this responsibility is referred to as a "duty." There are several different duties owed by the Trustee to the beneficiaries. If the Trustee breaches one or more of these duties, the trust beneficiaries may sue the Trustee for any damage caused by the breach.

## THE DUTY OF LOYALTY

A Trustee owes the beneficiaries a duty of absolute loyalty. The duty of loyalty includes the duty to avoid self-dealing (unless specifically allowed by the trust) and the duty of avoid conflicts of interest. Self-dealing occurs where the Trustee uses trust property for a purpose that benefits the Trustee rather than the beneficiaries.

California law does allow a Trustee to engage in self-dealing if the person who created the trust or all of the beneficiaries agree in writing to the transaction after the details of the proposed transaction are fully disclosed. A conflict of interest arises if the Trustee is considering dealing with another party in a transaction that may affect the Trustee's ability to properly assess the transaction.

For example, if the Trustee is allowed to sell trust property and hold the property for the beneficiaries, the Trustee would have a conflict of interest if the potential buyer was the Trustee's friend.

The main difference between self-dealing and a conflict of interest is that self-dealing benefits the Trustee, and a conflict of interest is something that could potentially cloud the Trustee's judgment with respect to the trust and its beneficiaries.

## THE DUTY OF PRUDENCE

In California, a Trustee is obligated to administer the trust property with a level of skill and care that a person of ordinary prudence would exercise if dealing with his or her own property. This is an objective standard, meaning that it is of no significance as to whether the Trustee thought he or she was acting prudently.

For example, if the trust directs the Trustee to invest some or all of the trust property, the duty of prudence would require the Trustee to investigate investment opportunities such as by conducting research and perhaps consulting with investment experts. The duty of prudence also requires the Trustee to spread the risk of loss by diversifying the trust investment, unless it would not be prudent to do so.

## THE DUTY TO BE IMPARTIAL

The duty of impartiality is designed to prevent the Trustee from favoring some beneficiaries over other beneficiaries. The duty commonly arises where the trust directs the Trustee to distribute income from trust property to some beneficiaries, and to then distribute the actual trust property after some period of time to remainder beneficiaries. In this situation, the beneficiaries entitled to income want the Trustee to invest the trust property in risky investments to maximize the accrued interest. Conversely, the remainder beneficiaries want the Trustee to invest the property in safe investments to protect the principal but produce little income. In this situation, the duty of loyalty may require the Trustee to invest the trust property so that it produces a reasonable income while preserving the property for the final remainder beneficiaries.

## THE DUTY TO COLLECT TRUST PROPERTY

A Trustee is required to collect trust property without unreasonable delay to protect that property. This duty may also require the Trustee to examine the trust property to ensure that the collected property is the property specified in the trust document. Collecting and identifying the trust property is also necessary to avoid the risk that the Trustee could mistake trust property for his own. Maintaining proper insurance coverage on some types of property is also advised (such as on real estate or vehicles).

## DUTY TO ENFORCE OR DEFEND CLAIMS RELATED TO THE TRUST

By way of example, if the trust is entitled to ownership or control of assets not properly held in trust title, or to damages (such as by way of a lawsuit related to the death of the trust Grantor), or to reimbursement by others for expenses paid, you have a duty to enforce these claims on behalf of the trust. With regard to claims against the trust, if someone sues the trust in an attempt to obtain ownership or control of trust assets, otherwise interferes with the proper administration of the trust, or contests the terms of the trust, you as the Trustee have a duty to defend against those claims. The expenses involved in enforcing or defending claims, including attorney and or professional fees, may usually be paid from the trust, unless your actions are unlawful or involve gross negligence or willful misconduct, and so long as the expenses are reasonable.

## DUTY OF CONFIDENTIALITY

The trust document and its records and accounting are to be kept confidential and only released to the beneficiaries of the trust or to whom you must give notice of certain action. Generally speaking, the trust document does not need to be filed with the Probate Court or Recorder's Office, or otherwise made public record. Obviously, from time to time, certain third-parties like your attorney, CPA or financial advisor may require access to confidential information. Tax authorities or real estate escrow or title companies may also require certain limited disclosures. You should always be cautious about revealing any confidential information and consult with your Estate Attorney first if you have any doubts as to whether a disclosure is appropriate.

## DUTY TO ACCOUNT TO THE BENEFICIARIES

Under the California Probate Code, there is a duty to provide an accounting to the beneficiaries of a trust that has now become irrevocable. That duty to account is at least once a year while the trust is left open. The Probate Code prescribes a very specific manner in which the accounting is to be provided and outlines the time limits within which a beneficiary may object to the accounting in Court. Your Estate Attorney should be able to help you prepare a trust accounting to serve on all of the trust beneficiaries.

# CHAPTER SEVEN

# Trust Record Keeping and Accountings

YOUR DUTY TO PREPARE an accounting for the beneficiaries will be dependent upon what the trust document says the standard is, as well as what California State law says. Your attorney should be able to help you identify the accounting standard that applies in your particular situation.

The default for the trust accounting standard if the trust is silent can be found in the California Probate Code. The Trustee must provide an accounting to the beneficiaries at least once a year. Circumstances may require an accounting more frequently, for example, when a new Trustee takes over.

The Trustee must deliver one final accounting after all administrative duties have been completed for the trust. However, a trust accounting is not required if the trust beneficiaries execute a waiver of their right to receive a periodic accounting for any given year one is required.

There are a number of legal requirements for trust accountings. For example, the accounting must notify the beneficiaries of any expenses incurred by the trust and any property distributed by the Trustee. There are many other requirements and it is wise to seek legal counsel to have the trust accounting properly prepared. If you do not provide an accounting when required to do so by law, as Trustee you can be sued by the trust beneficiaries.

Additionally, if you plan to receive compensation for acting as Trustee, the trust accounting must also include this information. However, make sure to ask your attorney what an appropriate Trustee fee is based upon your local jurisdiction. Also, keep in mind that the trustee fee is income and will need to be reported on your income tax return unless you waive taking a Trustee fee. Payment to CPAs and attorneys and any other expenses involved with the trust administration must also be disclosed in the accounting.

The accounting will also need to include special language informing each beneficiary that they have the right to ask the Court to review the accounting and that the beneficiaries have only three years to sue the Trustee if they think the Trustee acted improperly.

As Trustee, you will need to keep all records of any expenses paid from trust property as well as any bills paid out of pocket that you seek reimbursement for. Try to always write checks and keep copies of the checks used to support your accounting. This will also be helpful to provide to the professional who is preparing the official accounting.

An accurate list of all property owned by the trust and its value as of the date of death of the trust Grantor will be required for your CPA to file the final 1041 trust return or 706 estate tax return (when required or recommended). This information should also be shared with any beneficiaries when you are distributing assets directly to them such as real estate, stock or business interests that could have future capital gains consequences when sold. This is because there is typically a step-up in asset basis for capital gains taxes purposes in most estates. However, this is not always the case, so seeking advice from an experienced Estate Attorney and a CPA is highly recommended.

Lastly, you will want to maintain detailed records of every transaction and all bank statements related to the trust. This will help avoid misunderstandings or problems in the preparation of the accounting for the beneficiaries and protect you as Trustee from legal claims that you acted improperly in settling the trust estate.

# CHAPTER EIGHT

# How to Handle
# Non-Trust Assets

THERE ARE A FEW TYPES OF ASSETS that are not typically owned by a revocable trust. Some examples are IRAs, 401Ks, 403(b)s and other qualified retirement accounts. Life insurance policies and some annuity contracts are also often owned in the name of the decedent but should have a beneficiary associated with the policy or contract. Sometimes that beneficiary is the decedent's revocable trust.

There are other types of assets that may be non-trust assets simply because they were never funded to the trust by the trust Grantor intentionally or unintentionally. The most common asset we see this for is a bank account. If this is the case and there is no beneficiary statement attached to the bank account, there is typically a procedure we can take to get the bank to release funds through a special Affidavit to the Trustee of the trust so long as the total in assets outside the trust (without a beneficiary designation) totals less than $150,000 in California.

If the trust Grantor died with more than $150,000 in total in his or her name (not in trust title and without a beneficiary on the account) but the assets were listed on the trust asset schedule, there is a Petition that can be filed to get the assets re-titled to the name of the trust.

If the non-trusts assets combined are over $150,000, were not listed on the trust asset schedule and do not have beneficiary statements attached to them, a Probate Petition will usually be necessary to transfer the assets out of the name of the decedent to either the beneficiary of the decedent's will or to the decedent's natural heirs at law under the California Probate Code (if no will existed). Note that if the assets in the deceased's name were community property assets, there is a Spousal Property Petition that can be filed to transfer the assets to the spouse in some circumstances. However, if the Petition can be filed, this is a matter for a Probate Court Judge to decide and is not a guaranteed approval by the Court.

With regard to retirement accounts and life insurance policies, transfers of these types of assets are controlled by what is known as a beneficiary designation form. Regardless of what the decedent's trust or will says, the beneficiary of the retirement account or life insurance policy is controlled by the institution's beneficiary designation form, not the trust or will.

For a life insurance policy, there is usually a primary beneficiary and a contingent beneficiary listed on a form with the life insurance company that the policy owner filled out and signed at the time the policy was issued. Typically, a life insurance company will only discuss collection on a claim with whomever is designated on the beneficiary form. This may or may not be the decedent's revocable trust. If it is, it will be necessary for the Trustee to provide the life insurance company a copy of the death certificate, a certification of trust and the trust's tax ID number. The life insurance company will also most likely require you to fill out their insurance claim form.

If the trust was the beneficiary when the claim check arrives, make sure to retain a copy of the check and deposit the check to a bank account set up in the name of the trust with the new trust tax ID number (if a new tax I.D. number is required). For further information on whether or not you will need a new trust tax ID number for the trust, contact our office at (760) 448-2220 as it will depend upon the situation.

With regard to retirement accounts, if you are the surviving spouse of your spouse's account, you will likely want to investigate a spousal rollover to minimize income taxes. If your spouse was over the age of 70 at the time of death, make sure his or her required yearly minimum distribution has been withdrawn by the end of the year to avoid any penalties (for all non-Roth retirement accounts). If you are a non-spouse (i.e., child) beneficiary on the retirement account, make sure to consult with an Estate Attorney and CPA before making any withdrawals as there could be serious tax consequences (up to 48% loss of the account for California resident beneficiaries) if the account is liquidated.

# CHAPTER NINE

# When to Make Distributions to Beneficiaries

IN MOST CASES, the period of trust administration (which is the entire process of collecting and valuing assets and paying debts, expenses and taxes) takes anywhere from six months to a year and a half. We often advise our clients not to make any distributions out of the trust to beneficiaries until all matters related to the trust administration have concluded in order to limit any liability issues.

Upon the end of the trust administration however, the trust document itself will spell out and control when and how distributions to the beneficiaries are made. For example, when a trust calls for outright distributions to the beneficiaries, the trust will end upon conclusion of the trust administration. The assets that are left to a particular beneficiary in this case are re-titled into their name personally.

But if the trust creates a continuing trust for the benefit of a beneficiary, you must review the trust to see who the Trustee of that continuing trust will be and what rights the beneficiary has to demand income and/or principal from that Trustee.

The trust document may also provide for specific bequests to be distributed to particular beneficiaries. Typically, these bequests are to be satisfied prior to distribution of the residuary assets to the remainder beneficiaries of the trust.

The trust document must also be reviewed closely to determine to whom distributions will be made. For example, a named beneficiary may be deceased and if that is the case, you will need to determine who is the next in line to inherit that trust share or bequest under the provisions of the trust.

After you've determined who distributions are to be made to, the next step to determine is which assets will be distributed to each beneficiary. In most cases, each beneficiary will receive a share of what is remaining in the estate after the final payment of all debts and expenses. Such debts and expenses typically include professional fees for acting as a Trustee, last illness expenses, debts, attorneys fees, and accounting fees. Some other fees to consider are income taxes, both state and federal. In most cases, it's advisable to hold back a healthy reserve in a bank account for any potential income taxes that will be due in the next tax return filing period as well as fees due to the CPA for tax preparation.

A good CPA will be able to help you anticipate the estimated taxes that will be due and therefore you should be able to reserve an appropriate amount back. Should the tax liability be less than you've held in reserve, you may distribute the remaining balance to the trust beneficiaries after the taxes have been paid. Make sure to hold back a healthy reserve so that you don't have to try to recover any shortfall for taxes from distributions already made to beneficiaries.

If the trust doesn't specify specific dollar amounts or specific assets to be distributed to particular beneficiaries, it is typically in the Trustee's discretion to determine what type of assets will be distributed to each beneficiary. It's often advisable to meet and confer with the beneficiaries to get an idea of who may want what, particularly when it comes to tangible personal property. In the end, a beneficiary settlement agreement can be drawn up and executed by all beneficiaries to memorialize the agreement and reduce the risk of later litigation and liability to the Trustee.

With regard to personal property that is owned by the trust, as Trustee, you will need to consult the trust document for any specific bequests of specific property or to see if a Personal Property Memorandum existed listing items of a personal nature to be distributed to particular people. If there are no specific bequests and the personal property is owned by the trust, the Trustee will need to determine how best to distribute the personal property among the designated beneficiaries of the trust. If a consensus cannot be made with the beneficiaries, the Trustee typically may sell the personal property assets and distribute the proceeds from those assets to the beneficiaries at the close of the trust administration.

As mentioned earlier in this book, there may be assets that are passing outside the trust that need special attention. Examples in this category are life insurance, retirement benefits, IRAs and annuity contracts. Most likely, these types of assets will pass according to a beneficiary designation form outside the trust and directly to the named beneficiaries. However, in some cases they may flow to a trust (sometimes other than the Grantor's revocable trust). For example, the Grantor may also have a Retirement Plan Trust which is the designated beneficiary of their IRA(s).

It's also highly recommended to consult with a qualified Estate Attorney and accountant before any withdrawals are made from any IRA or other retirement account. There can be significant adverse income tax consequences if distributions are made from these types of accounts without proper advance consideration.

Another issue to consider before wrapping up trust administration and distributing funds to all the beneficiaries is whether or not you plan to take a Trustee fee (assuming the trust provides for a Trustee fee to the Trustee). The amount of Trustee fees you may take may also be limited by the trust document. If you do get paid Trustee fees, these will be taxable income to you. The bulk of your Trustee fees should usually be paid at the end of the trust administration. Your fees may also not be excessive and must be reasonably related to the nature of the amount of work you performed. You should consult an attorney regarding the proper amount of your fees and timing of their payment.

One final note, it is always advisable for the Trustee to obtain a written receipt from each beneficiary when a distribution is made. This will ensure that if a claim is ever made that they did not receive their distribution, you will have proof that the distribution occurred.

# CHAPTER TEN

# *About the Author*

BRENDA GEIGER is the Founder and CEO of Geiger Law Office, P.C. Geiger Law Office, P.C. is a Trusts & Estates law firm which began in 2007 in North County San Diego. The firm has helped thousands of families to protect themselves and their wealth through innovative estate  and asset protection strategies as well as trust administration services. The firm is also host to an annual Trusts & Estates Symposium each May that provides leading edge education to allied professionals and the firm's clients and sponsors a charity event to support the American Cancer Society each year in December.

While studying at the University of San Diego School of Law, Brenda was honored to be selected for the Oxford University International Comparative Law Program in Oxford England and was a member of the Entrepreneurship Clinic and San Diego International Law Journal.

Brenda is the author of six other books including *Safeguarding the Nest, Forth Edition, Secrets of Great Estate Planning, Third Edition, Protecting an Aging Parent from a Long Term Care Financial Crisis, Protecting Your Children's IRA Inheritance with a Retirement Protector Trust, Protecting You and Your Business*, and *Estate Planning Secrets of the Affluent*.

Brenda is also a sought-after speaker, coach and attorney on a variety of business, estate and asset protection topics. She has been featured on KPBS, NBC, KFMB 760, North County Lawyer Magazine, Wealth Counsel Magazine, and the San Diego International Law Journal.

On a more personal note, Brenda grew up in the mid-west, married the love of her life Len, a former Marine Corps officer in 2004, and has a son and a daughter that she loves to spend time with. The Geigers love adventure, soccer and travel and look forward to many more years of it.

You can connect with Brenda at www.geigerlawoffice.com or at https://www.linkedin.com/in/brendageiger/.

# CHAPTER ELEVEN

# Glossary of Trust Administration Terms

**Accumulation Trust**: A type of trust, usually within a Retirement Plan Trust, that permits assets to build up in a sub-trust for a beneficiary over time rather than requiring the assets to be distributed immediately through a Conduit in the trust.

**Advanced Estate Planning**: Techniques that are designed to maximize benefits to your heirs and provide creditor protection while minimalizing or eliminating income and estate taxes. Also ensures that your wishes regarding estate distributions are followed as closely as possible.

**Annual Exclusion Gifting Trusts**: An irrevocable trust in which an annual amount of money may be transferred by gift to the trust without incurring a gift tax or eating into the Grantor's unified credit. This amount can be transferred in the form of cash or other assets and may be aggregated by the number of beneficiaries. In 2018, the annual gift tax exclusion amount is $15,000 per beneficiary.

**Annuity Payments:** A series of payments made at fixed intervals of time.

**Beneficiary**: A person, charity, or entity that derives advantage from something, especially a trust, will, retirement account, annuity contract, or life insurance policy.

**Bypass Trust (aka "B" Trust):** A type of trust that allows a Grantor of the trust to provide for a surviving spouse for their lifetime and have their federal estate tax exemption allocated to that spousal trust. It can also help the Grantor to maintain control of how the trust assets are distributed after the death of the surviving spouse. Income, and sometimes principal, is generated from the trust assets and given to the surviving spouse to ensure he or she is provided for until death for his or her health, education, maintenance and support.

**Cascading Trust:** A type of continuing trust where by the assets cascade or transfer from one generation to the next or from one set of beneficiaries to the next upon the happening of a specific event (i.e., at the death of the initial generation).

**Charitable Lead Trust**: An irrevocable trust that allows certain benefits to go to a charity and the remainder to your beneficiaries upon death.

**Charitable Remainder Annuity Trust**: A planned giving trust where a donor places a major gift of property into a trust. The trust then pays a fixed amount of income each year to the donor or the donor's specified beneficiary. When the donor dies, the remainder of the trust is transferred to a named charity.

**Charitable Remainder Trust**: An irrevocable trust that allows you to receive an income stream for a defined period of time and stipulate that any remainder go to a charity.

**Charitable Remainder Uni-trust**: An irrevocable trust created under the authority of Internal Revenue Code § 664. This special, irrevocable trust (known as a "CRUT") has two primary characteristics: 1) Once established, the CRUT distributes a fixed percentage of the value of its assets (on an annual or more frequent basis) to a non-charitable beneficiary (which is considered the Settlor of the trust); and 2) At the expiration of a specified time (usually the death of the Settlor), the remaining balance of the CRUT's assets are distributed to a named charity.

**Completed Gift**: A gift in which the dominion and control of the property is placed beyond the donor's reach.

**Conduit Trust**: A type of trust, usually within a Retirement Plan Trust, in which an IRA annual required minimum distribution simply passes through the trust and gets paid out immediately to the beneficiary of the trust on an annual basis.

**Contingent Remainder Interest**: An interest, which will go to a person or entity only upon a certain set of circumstances existing at the time the title-holder dies.

**Domestic Asset Protection Trust (DAPT)**: A self-settled trust in which funds are held on a discretionary basis by a third-party Trustee with the Grantor typically being a beneficiary of the trust. These trusts are most commonly set up in order to mitigate taxes and penetration by a future creditor, divorcing spouse, lawsuit, or bankruptcy. Various state statutes and case law govern the effectiveness of self-settled DAPT trusts.

**Dynasty Trust**: A trust designed to eliminate or minimize estate taxes with each transfer to subsequent generations. With the trust as owner of the assets and by making defined distributions to each generation, the assets of the trust are not subject to estate taxes to each successive generation.

**Federal Estate and Gift Tax Unified Credit**: This is the amount expressed as a total amount for estate, gift and generation-skipping transfer tax exemption (the amount that is not taxed)— $11,400,000 million per person (2019)—and it is possible to use this exclusion to transfer assets by gift to another.

**Federal Estate Tax**: The estate tax is a tax on your right to transfer property at your death. It consists of an accounting of everything you own at your date of death. The federal estate tax exemption in 2018 is approximately $11,180,000 million per person with estate values above this subject to 40% federal estate tax.

**Federal Gift Tax**: If you give someone money or property during your lifetime, you may be subject to federal gift tax. Gifts above $15,000 (2019) are reportable to the IRS and will be deducted from your federal unified credit, which is approximately $11,400,000 million in 2018.

**Fiduciary:** Involving a position of trust and financial responsibility, especially with regard to the relationship between a Trustee and a beneficiary.

**Generation-skipping Transfer Tax**: An additional 40% estate tax on both outright gifts and transfers in trust to or for the benefit of unrelated persons who are more than 37.5 years younger than the donor or to related persons more than one generation younger than the donor, such as grandchildren.

**Grantor**: The creator of a trust, and usually the individual whose assets are put into the trust.

**Grantor Retained Annuity Trust (GRAT):** An irrevocable trust typically funded by gifts from its Grantor and designed to shift future appreciation on quickly appreciating assets to the next generation during the Grantor's lifetime.

**"Grantor" Trust Status**: Trust provisions in which the Grantor, the creator of the trust, retains one or more powers over the trust and because of this, the trust's income is taxable to the Grantor.

**Independent Trustee**: A person or entity that has no beneficial interest, present or future, vested or contingent, direct or indirect, in the trust.

**Interested Trustee**: An individual Trustee who is a current beneficiary of the original trust or to whom the net income or principal of the original trust would be distributed if the original trust were terminated.

**Irrevocable Gifting Trust**: A trust where the Grantor gifts money or other assets to the trust and gives up all right, title and interest in the property that is transferred for the benefit of children, grandchildren, or other beneficiaries.

**Irrevocable Life Insurance Trust (ILIT)**: A type of irrevocable trust that is specifically designed to own life insurance. Once the ILIT has been set up, you will transfer ownership of your life insurance policies to the Trustee of the ILIT.

**Irrevocable Trust**: A trust that cannot be terminated or revoked or otherwise modified or amended by the Grantor. As modern trust law continues to evolve, however, it may be possible to affect changes to irrevocable trusts through court actions, a process called decanting, which allows the assets of an existing irrevocable trust to be transferred to a new trust with different provisions, or through the use of a Trust Protector.

**Lifetime Gift Exemption**: The amount you can transfer to others (U.S. citizens) during your lifetime without implication of a gift tax, $15,000 per recipient (2018).

**Limited Liability Company (LLC)**: A hybrid business entity having certain characteristics of both a corporation and a partnership or sole proprietorship (depending on how many owners there are). An LLC, although a business entity, is a type of unincorporated association and is not a corporation. The primary characteristic an LLC shares with a corporation is limited liability, and the primary characteristic it shares with a partnership is the availability of pass-through income taxation. It is often more flexible than a corporation, and it is well-suited for companies with a single owner and rental real estate holdings.

**Perpetual Trust**: A type of trust that passes from generation to generation so that the children and grandchildren of the original beneficiaries can also benefit from the trust.

**Perpetuity**: To go on forever.

**Qualified Personal Residence Trust (QPRT)**: A specific type of trust that allows its creator to put a primary residence or vacation home into the trust for the primary purpose of reducing the gift and estate tax of the trust creator, or to secure creditor protection for the home when transferring the property to a beneficiary.

**Qualified Terminable Interest Property Trust (QTIP Trust):** A type of trust that allows the Grantor of the trust to provide for a surviving spouse. It also helps the Grantor to maintain control of how the trust assets are distributed after the death of the surviving spouse. Income, and sometimes principal, is generated from the trust assets and given to the surviving spouse to ensure he or she is provided for until death.

**Remainder Interest:** A future interest given to a person or charity (referred to as the transferee or remainderman) capable of becoming the owner (or one benefiting) when the primary beneficial interest ends.

**Required Minimum Distribution:** This is the minimum amount you must withdraw from your retirement account each year.

**Retirement Protector Trust (aka "Retirement Plan Trust"):** A revocable or irrevocable trust that is drafted to be either the primary or contingent beneficiary of a retirement account or several retirement accounts. The trust is designed to allow a successor Trustee to stretch out a retirement account on behalf of one or more of the beneficiaries of the trust and provide creditor protection of the retirement account(s) for the beneficiaries after they inherit them.

**Revocable Living Trust**: A trust in which you transfer ownership of your property into a trust throughout the course of your lifetime, select beneficiaries and revoke or terminate the trust at your discretion.

**Revocable Trust**: A trust created during a lifetime over which the Grantor reserves the right to terminate, revoke, modify, or amend the trust agreement.

**Spendthrift Trust**: A trust provision restricting both voluntary and involuntary transfers of a beneficiary's interest, frequently in order to protect assets from claims of the beneficiary's creditors.

**Survivor's Trust (aka "A" Trust)**: A type of trust formed after the death of the first spouse in a joint trust that leaves all of the deceased spouse's half of the community property and any separate property he or she owned at death to a survivor's trust. The surviving spouse has complete access and control over the survivor's trust and may withdraw assets or change the eventual beneficiaries of the trust by amendment.

**Trustee**: Any person or entity that holds property, authority, or a position of trust or responsibility for the benefit of another.

**Trust Protector**: A person or entity who can make certain limited changes to the trust, such as fill in a Trustee vacancy, interpret trust terms, move the administration of the trust to a new state, or grant certain powers to the Trustee or to a beneficiary.

**706 Death Tax Return**: An IRS tax form used for reporting the values of the assets held by the deceased tax payer where the federal estate tax and generation-skipping transfer (GST) tax allocations can be made in relation to property transferred to beneficiaries.

**709 Gift Tax Return**: An IRS tax form used for transfers subject to the federal gift and certain generation-skipping transfer (GST) taxes, and for allocation of the lifetime GST exemption to property transferred during the transferor's lifetime.

# GEIGER LAW OFFICE, P.C.

www.geigerlawoffice.com

1917 Palomar Oaks Way, Suite 160
Carlsbad, CA 92008

**(760) 448-2220**

*and*

16A Journey, Suite. 200
Aliso Viejo, CA 92656

**(949) 769-2440**

WA

Made in the USA
Columbia, SC
01 September 2024

40904473R00037